MY FIRST BOOK

CROATIA

ALL ABOUT CROATIA FOR KIDS

GL BED
CHILDREN BOOKS

Interior and cover Design: Daniel Day
Editor: Margaret Bam

For My Sons, Daniel, David and Jude

Dubrovnik, Croatia

Croatia

Croatia is a **country**.

A country is land that is controlled by a **single government**. Countries are also called **nations, states, or nation-states**.

Countries can be **different sizes**. Some countries are big and others are small.

Dubrovnik, Croatia

Where Is Croatia?

Croatia is located in the continent of Europe.

A continent is a massive area of land that is separated from others by water or other natural features.

Croatia is situated at the crossroads of Central and Southeast Europe.

Zagreb, Croatia

Capital

The capital of Croatia is **Zagreb.**

Zagreb is located in the **north-western part** of the country.

Zagreb is the largest city in Croatia.

Trogir, Croatia

Regions

Croatia is a country that is made up of 5 regions.

The regions of Croatia are as follows:

Mainland, Dalmatia, Kvarner, Istria, Slavonia.

Rovinj, Istria, Croatia

Population

Croatia has population of around 4 **million people** making it the 128th most populated country in the world and the 27th most populated country in Europe.

Size

Croatia is **56,594 square kilometres** making it the 26th largest country in Europe by area.

Croatia is the 124th largest country in the world.

Languages

The official language of Croatia is **Croatian.** The Croatian language originated in Croatia and is spoken by over 5 million people worldwide.

Here are a few phrases in Croatian
- **Bok** - Hello
- **Drago mi je** - Nice to meet you
- **Kako si?** - How are you?
- **Hvala** - Thank you

Pula Arena, Pula, Croatia

Attractions

There are lots of interesting places to see in Croatia.

Some beautiful places to visit in Croatia are

- Plitvice Lakes National Park
- Diocletian's Palace
- Krka National Park
- Golden Horn Beach
- Pula Arena
- Sea Organ

Rovinj, Croatia

History of Croatia

People have lived in Croatia for a very long time. It is believed that humans have inhabited Croatia throughout the prehistoric times.

Tomislav was the first king of Croatia. Croatia was declared independent on 25 June 1991 and on 8 October 1991, the Croatian Parliament severed all remaining ties with Yugoslavia.

Pula, Croatia

Customs in Croatia

Croatia has many fascinating customs and traditions.

- **Croatians are very sociable and hospitable. It is common for Croatians to visit friends and family unannounced.**
- **Coffee plays an important part in Croatian culture. Many people socialise over a cup of coffee.**

Waterfall in Krka National Park, Croatia

Music of Croatia

There are many different music genres in Croatia such as **Klapa, Turbo-folk, Éntekhno, and Croatian hip hop.**

Some notable Croatian musicians include
- **Nina Badrić**
- **Gibonni**
- **Marko Perković Thompson**
- **Severina**
- **Jelena Rozga**
- **Tony Cetinski**

Peka with mix meat and vegetables

Food of Croatia

Croatia is known for its delicious, flavoursome and diverse food.

The national dish of Croatia is **Zagorski štrukli** which is composed of dough and various types of filling which can be either boiled or baked and sweet or savoury.

Food of Croatia

Some popular dishes in Croatia include

- Crni rižot
- Fritule
- Gregada
- Ispod peke
- Istrian truffles
- Kulen sausage
- Kvarner scampi
- Olive oil.

Plitvice Lakes, Croatia

Weather in Croatia

Croatia has a Mediterranean climate, with mild and wet winters and hot, dry summers.

The warmest months are **July and August.**

Hvar Town, Hvar, Croatia

Animals of Croatia

There are many wonderful animals in Croatia.

Here are some animals that live in Croatia

- Wolves
- Bears
- Foxes
- Wild boars
- Weasels
- Wild cats

Stiniva Beach

Beaches

There are many beautiful beaches in Croatia which is one of the reasons why so many people visit this beautiful country every year.

Here are some of Croatia's beaches

- Murvica
- Borak
- Bačvice
- Zlatni Rat
- Punta Rata

Southern Dalmatia, Croatia

Sports of Croatia

Sports play an integral part in Croatian culture. The most popular sport is **Football.**

Here are some of famous sportspeople from Croatia

- **Goran Ivanišević - Tennis**
- **Toni Kukoč - Basketball**
- **Niko Kovač - Football**
- **Blanka Vlašić - Athletics**

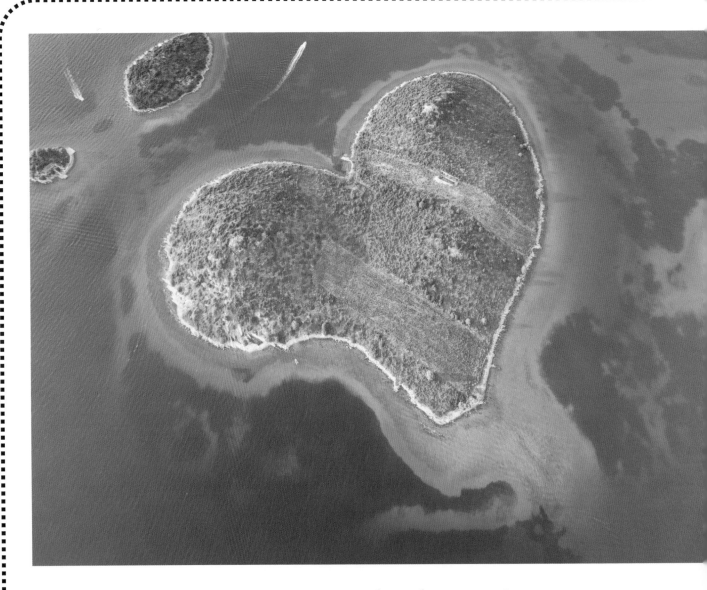

Heart Love Island, Croatia

Famous

Many successful people hail from Croatia.

Here are some notable Croatian figures

- **Janica Kostelic – Skier**
- **Sandra Perkovic – Athlete**
- **Mirko Filipovic – Martial Artist**
- **Nikola Tesla – Inventor**
- **Rudjer Boskovic – Physicist**

Fort St. John, Dubrovnik, Croatia

Something Extra...

As a little something extra, we are going to share some lesser known facts about Croatia.

- **Croatia is home of the world's biggest truffle.**
- **Gladiators used to fight in Croatia.**
- **Croatia is home to the world's smallest town.**

Words From the Author

We hope that you enjoyed learning about the wonderful country of Croatia.

Croatia is a country rich in culture and beauty, with lots of wonderful places to visit and people to meet.

We hope you continue to learn more about this wonderful nation. If you enjoyed this book, consider leaving a review!

With Love

Printed in Great Britain
by Amazon

26348130R00027